To Zinnia, my daughter — S.B.

To Manuel Gutiérrez Lobeto, my grandpa, who helped me
pick all the leaves I wanted to when I was a kid. — I.M.

Library of Congress Control Number: 2023932919
ISBN 9781959244011

Text copyright © 2023 by Stephen Briseño
Illustrations by Isabel Muñoz
Illustrations copyright © 2023 The Innovation Press

Published by The Innovation Press
7511 Greenwood Avenue N. #4132, Seattle, WA 98103
www.theinnovationpress.com

Printed and bound by Worzalla
Production date June 2023

Cover art by Isabel Muñoz
Book layout by Tim Martyn

QUEEN OF LEAVES

THE STORY OF BOTANIST YNES MEXIA

WRITTEN BY
STEPHEN BRISEÑO

ILLUSTRATED BY
ISABEL MUÑOZ

The wax palm knows what it's like to be lonely.

It grows where most think a palm tree shouldn't—high on the mountains of South America.

Ynes Mexia knew what it was like to be lonely, too.

Ynes's family lived like plants in separate pots.
Father busy with work in Washington, DC. Mother
and sister, Adele, rubbing elbows with the wealthy.

And Ynes? She was alone with her books, in the shade of trees.

The wax palm knows how to adapt.

As the land rose to become the towering peaks of the Andes, it learned to live in harsher, colder conditions.

When the love between Father and Mother wilted, Ynes and Adele moved to Philadelphia with Mother.

Ynes floated between boarding schools, unable
to connect with the other girls, waiting for letters
from Father in Mexico City.
Letters that never came.

The wax palm knows what it's like to carry scars.

Every year, it sheds its leaves, creating dark circles that stain its trunk.

After high school, Father invited Ynes to live with him. A chance to know Father better!

But when she arrived, Ynes was more servant than daughter—handling cooks, arranging gardeners, and planning banquets.

When Father died, he gave Ynes his ranches in Mexico and Texas. Ynes now owned it all.

However, with troubled marriages and a difficult business to run . . .

Ynes broke down.

Ynes moved to San Francisco where a doctor encouraged her to experience life fully.

And so Ynes returned to an old friend: the great outdoors.

She was captured by the majestic peaks of the Sierra Nevada.

Enchanted by the mighty California redwood.

So much so, she helped protect California's natural beauty.

The wax palm knows what it's like to stick out.

With its striped trunk and a burst of green fronds, it looks like it's from another planet.

Ynes enrolled in college when she was fifty-one years old. Her classmates were thirty years younger!

Ynes did not care.

Her favorite class was botany, the study of plants. Every plant was a promise. Each seed a possibility.

And when Ynes had the opportunity to join an expedition to collect plant samples in Mexico, she jumped at the chance for adventure.

The wax palm knows how to gather the rare and beautiful.

Many birds, like the endangered yellow-eared parrot, find safety in its dead leaves and feast on its fruit.

Back in Mexico, Ynes used her Spanish to her advantage, learning where to find unique plants from locals.

Ynes trekked for hours in the foothills gathering specimens,

climbing rocky waterfalls,

sleeping in barns beneath the stars,

tumbling off cliffs—and breaking a few ribs on the way down.

Collecting plants required lugging a heavy press and supplies in the hot sun, far away from life's comforts. Each sample had to be plucked, prepared, and pressed. It was difficult work.

Ynes would not have had it any other way.

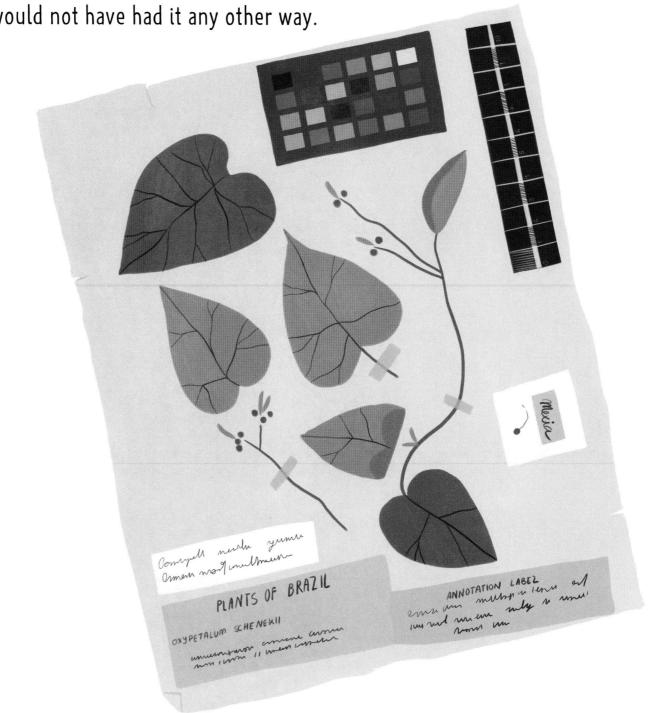

The wax palm knows what it's like to reach for the clouds.

To gain such height, it must wait, focusing its energy on strengthening its trunk. But when its time comes, it shoots up strong.

Society thought women should not lead a life of adventure or travel alone. Ynes thought otherwise.

On her first solo trip to Mexico, Ynes collected 5,000 samples.

On the next trip, she collected over 33,000.

On a yearlong trip to Central America, she rounded up 65,000 specimens!

A few new species she discovered were even named after her, like the daisy *Mexianthus mexicanus.*

Impressed by her work, museums and universities asked Ynes to collect plants for them. Her fame as a botanical collector was taking root.

The wax palm knows what it's like to be in danger.

After years of having wax scraped off to make candles, leaves cut for Palm Sunday services, and entire trees chopped down, the wax palm is now endangered.

Ynes's adventures often put her in scary situations.

Lost in the snowy Denali wilderness, Ynes was rescued by an Alaskan and his sled dogs.

On a mountainside in Brazil, she slept in a tent made of alligator skin while rain hammered down.

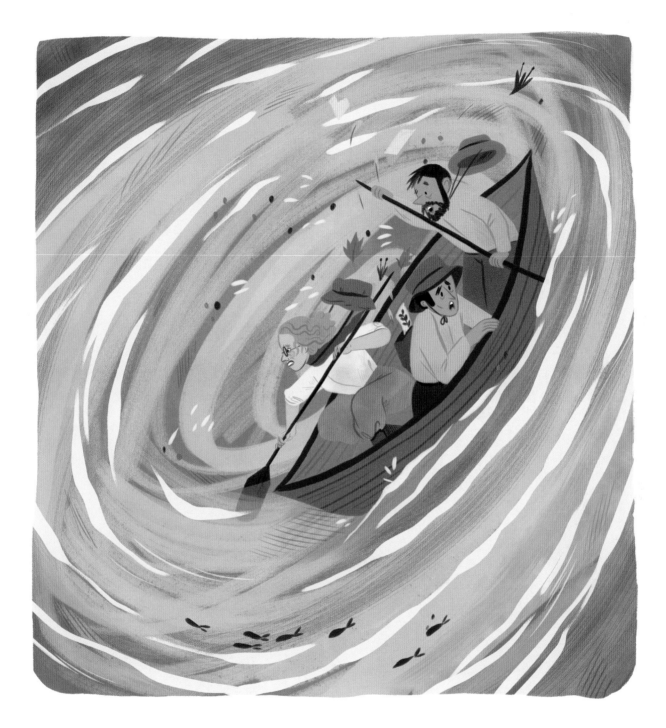

Canoeing the Amazon River, her group became trapped in a whirlpool, her specimens—her life—nearly lost to the murky waters.

Ynes began her pursuit of the mysterious wax palm at the age of sixty-four. She had to find this palm that grew in such unique, harsh conditions—which led her to Ecuador.

With drenching rain, thick mud, and even an earthquake, this expedition proved more challenging to Ynes than any before.

She loaded up her pack,

mounted her horse,

and kept going,

up and up, higher and higher,

until finally she found it:

a wax palm splitting the sky some two hundred feet above, with fronds so large it took two men to lift them.

On the way back, Ynes ate what she thought were blueberries. Bent over with terrible pain, she soon realized they were poisonous.

To save her from a most unpleasant death, her guides used an odd remedy: a freshly plucked chicken feather to tickle her throat.

She threw up all the berries, and by morning, Ynes was her unstoppable self.

The wax palm leaves a legacy.

Thanks to Ynes, it is now the national tree of Colombia.

Ynes continues to influence generations of botanists and scientists. Exploring the world from Denali to Tierra del Fuego, she gifted to science over 150,000 specimens and an entire new genus of plants.

And thanks to Ynes and others she inspired, the wax palm now has efforts in place to preserve its unique beauty.

Ynes proved that there wasn't any place, any field of study, or any age at which a woman could not excel.

She didn't always know what it was like to be accepted.

Or to have friends.

Or to feel important.

But Ynes did know what it was like to be

a trailblazer,

a groundbreaker,

a late bloomer.

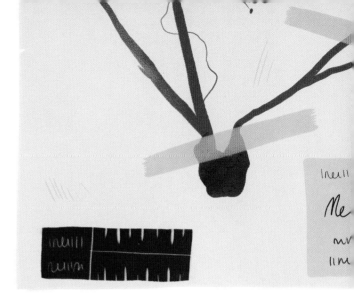

The wax palm knows what it's like to defy the odds.

Ynes Mexia knew it, too.

AUTHOR'S NOTE

While researching Ynes Mexia, I often find myself leaning back in my chair, rereading certain paragraphs, astonished at what I just learned. This woman was an adventurer extraordinaire! Ynes was like Indiana Jones, trekking around the globe to exotic, faraway destinations. But she wasn't a fictional character. She breathed, struggled, and lived life to the fullest. She was a human being with hopes and dreams, flaws and imperfections. Just like you and me.

Ynes overcame incredible odds during her lifetime. The first part of her life was clouded in loneliness, pain, and a lack of direction. Family troubles, a distant father, death, divorce, mental pain. It was enough to break just about anyone.

If Ynes had not taken the risk to move to San Francisco, her story would have ended in Mexico. Two people had an immense impact on Ynes: Dr. Phillip K. Brown and Alice Eastwood. Dr. Brown saw the value of mental health far ahead of the times and was her friend for the rest of his life. Alice Eastwood was a trailblazer like Ynes, a self-taught botanist in a male-dominated field who made a name for herself. Both encouraged Ynes to find her place in the world and to pursue her passion.

Even though her career did not start until much later in life, she wouldn't let anyone look down on her because of her age or gender. She did what made her heart sing, and the world is a richer place for it.

As a father, I want my daughter to be like Ynes: fearless, brave, and having the grit and determination to overcome the most formidable obstacles. I hope you, dear reader, after reading Ynes's story, aspire to the same.

Stephen Briseño
San Antonio, Texas

BIBLIOGRAPHY

Anema, Durlynn. *The Perfect Specimen: The 20th Century Renown Botanist, Ynés Mexía*. Parker, CO: National Writers Press, 2019.

Anema, Durlynn. *Ynes Mexia: Botanist and Adventurer*. Greensboro, NC: Morgan Reynolds Pub., 2005.

Bond, Louie. "Wild Women.: Seeds of Knowledge: Ynes Mexia and Maude Young." *Texas Parks & Wildlife*, March 2020. https://tpwmagazine.com/archive/2020/mar/wildwomen/index.phtml.

Candeias, Matt. "The Tallest of Palms." *In Defense of Plants* (blog). April 16, 2015. https://www.indefenseofplants.com/blog/2015/4/15/the-tallest-of-palms.

Global Trees Campaign. "Quindío Wax Palm." Accessed March 31, 2023. https://globaltrees.org/threatened-trees/trees/ceroxylon-quindiuense.

Harteau, Adam and Emily. "Photos: Exploring the World's Tallest Palm Tree Forest." *Condé Nast Traveler*, February 25, 2015. https://www.cntraveler.com/galleries/2015-02-25/photos-exploring-the-worlds-tallest-palm-tree-forest-valle-de-cocora-colombia.

Nadler, Susie. "Rare Andean Wax Palm Grows Here in SF, and Almost Nowhere Else." Flora Grubb Gardens. January 6, 2020. https://www.floragrubb.com/whats-new-at-flora-grubb-gardens/rare-andean-wax-palm-grows-here-in-sf-and-almost-nowhere-else-in-the-world.

Pedry, Sarah. "Ynes Mexia and the Search for the Elusive Palm." *The Hairpin*, June 28, 2017. https://www.thehairpin.com/2017/06/scenes-and-sketches-americas-women-naturalists-2/.

Sanín, María J., and Gloria Galeano. "A Revision of the Andean Wax Palms, *Ceroxylon* (Arecaceae)." *Phytotaxa* 34. Auckland, New Zealand: Magnolia Press, 2011.

Shekhar, Akarsh. "Ynés Mexia: Many Don't Realize How Much We Owe to This Botanist." *DailyHawker*, November 6, 2020. https://www.dailyhawker.co.uk/ynes-mexia-many-dont-realize-how-much-we-owe-to-this-botanist.

Sherriff, Lucy. "'Living Corpses': Why Colombia's National Tree Is at Risk." *BBC News*, November 5, 2018. https://www.bbc.com/news/world-latin-america-45901218.

Siber, Kate. "How Finding Rare Plants Saved Ynes Mexia's Life." *Outside*, February 20, 2019. https://www.outsideonline.com/outdoor-adventure/exploration-survival/ynes-mexia-plant-collector/.

Smith, Jennie Erin. "Stalking the Endangered Wax Palm." *New York Times*, November 5, 2019. https://www.nytimes.com/2019/11/05/science/colombia-wax-palms-biodiversity.html.

"Wax Palms of Cocora Valley." *Atlas Obscura*, March 19, 2018. https://www.atlasobscura.com/places/wax-palms-of-cocora-valley.

Wikipedia. "Ceroxylon Quindiuense." Wikimedia Foundation. Last modified March 29, 2023. https://en.wikipedia.org/wiki/Ceroxylon_quindiuense.

"Ynés Mexía: Mexican-American Botanist and Adventurer | Unladylike2020 | American Masters | PBS." American Masters PBS, March 31, 2020. YouTube. https://www.youtube.com/watch?v=l09r6811cGo.

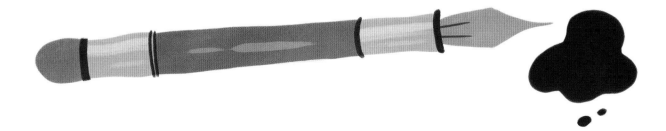

Mexia

PLANTS OF BRAZIL

OXYPETALUM SCHENEKII